ROBERT LOUIS STEVENSON
TREASURE ISLAND

essay by
Trevor Pickering M.A. & M. Phil.
Columbia University

Treasure Island

art by Alex Blum
adaptation by Ken Fitch
cover by Tommy Lee Edwards

For Classics Illustrated Study Guides
computer recoloring by VanHook Studios
editor: Madeleine Robins
assistant editor: Gregg Sanderson
design: Scott Friedlander

Classics Illustrated: Treasure Island © Twin Circle Publishing Co.,
a division of Frawley Enterprises; licensed to First Classics, Inc.
All new material and compilation © 1997 by Acclaim Books, Inc.

Dale-Chall R.L.: 7.7

ISBN 1-57840-031-7

Classics Illustrated® is a registered trademark of the Frawley Corporation.

Acclaim Books, New York, NY
Printed in the United States

STUDY GUIDE

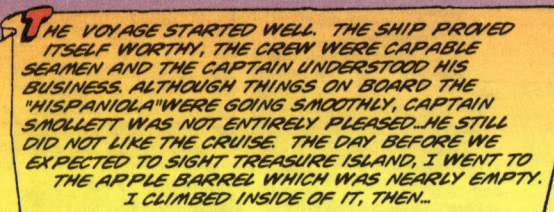

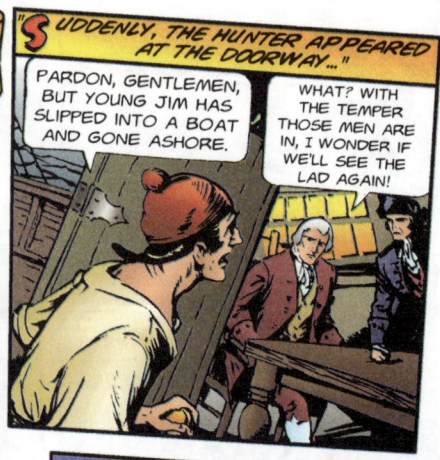

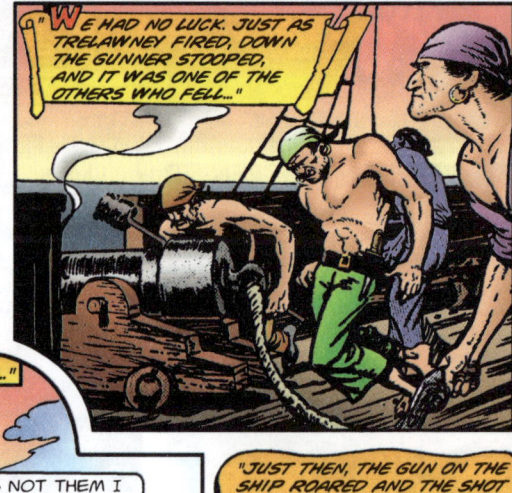

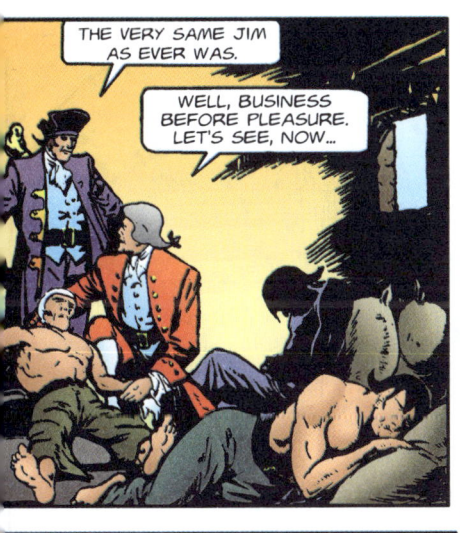

THE shortage of man-power kept everyone busy and the trip passed quickly. Finally, the "Hispaniola" put into a South American port to take on new hands...

WHAT DO YOU SAY TO A NIGHT ON SHORE?

FINE! I'D LOVE TO SEE A TOWN AGAIN AFTER LIVING ON TREASURE ISLAND!

WHEN WE RETURNED EARLY NEXT MORNING...

JOHN SILVER'S GONE. HE STOLE AWAY LAST NIGHT WITH A SACK FULL OF GOLD.

WE'RE LUCKY TO BE RID OF HIM SO CHEAPLY.

WITH new hands on board, the voyage home was a good one, and it was a happy crew that finally saw the port of Bristol...and the end of the cruise to Treasure Island...

We all had a share of the Treasure. Captain Smollett retired from the Sea... Gray saved his money and became part owner of a fine Ship. Ben Gunn spent his small fortune in just nineteen days and went to keep a Lodge in the country. Of John Silver, we've heard no more. That formidable seaman, with one leg, has at last gone out of my Life.

Jim Hawkins

THE END.

TREASURE ISLAND
ROBERT LOUIS STEVENSON

The Author

Robert Louis Stevenson, Scottish novelist, essayist, and poet, is best remembered for his adventure classics *Treasure Island* and *Kidnapped*, and for his fantastic tale *Dr. Jekyll and Mr. Hyde*.

Robert Louis Balfour Stevenson was born in Edinburgh on November 13, 1850. His father, grandfather, and two of his uncles were engineers who specialized in lighthouse design. Young Robert was a sickly child, suffering from tubercular symptoms that affected his stamina and strength. His illness made for an irregular education. He spent much of his childhood traveling to climates that were good for his health, and therefore got most of his schooling from private tutors along the way. Eventually Stevenson entered Edinburgh University. To please his family, he tried to study engineering, but later on he opted for the study of law. Although he was admitted to the bar in 1875, he never practiced. Instead, he was drawn more and more to writing. Stevenson rejected the strict Presbyterianism of his family and began to keep company with  artists, writers, and a generally more Bohemian crowd. At the age of twenty Stevenson revealed to his family his desire to be a writer, much to their disappointment.

In 1876, during a trip to France, Stevenson met Fanny Van der Grift Osborne, an American woman who was separated from her husband and two children. When Fanny returned to San Francisco, Stevenson followed her there to be with her after the divorce, and the two were married in May, 1880. Stevenson, still ill, lived on an allowance provided by his father, and the couple used the funds to travel to various

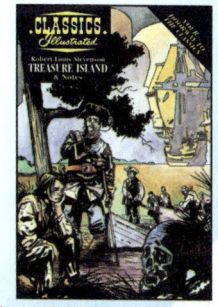

European and American health resorts. Shortly after Stevenson completed a successful treatment of his illness at a resort in the Adirondack Mountains of New York State in 1887, Stevenson's father died, leaving his son a large inheritance. With their new financial freedom, Stevenson and his family made an eighteen-month voyage to the South Seas. They visited such places as the Marquesas, Tahiti, Australia, and Samoa, which provided scenery for much of Stevenson's later work.

Finally, in 1889, Stevenson bought an estate on the Samoan island of Upolu, calling it Vailima. There Stevenson lived his remaining years, writing essays and fiction. He also spent much of his time fighting against the colonial exploitation of the Samoan islands, which gained him respect among the islanders. When he died of a cerebral hemorrhage on December 3, 1894, the island population cleared a trail through the jungle to the summit of Mt. Vaea, where Stevenson had asked to be buried.

Writing *Treasure Island*

Treasure Island, Stevenson's first successful publication, was begun in 1881 in Scotland. Interestingly, the novel originated with a map of two imaginary islands that Stevenson had drawn for his stepson. He called the larger island Treasure Island and the smaller one which nestled in its southeast shores Skeleton Island. Stevenson began to invent a story about the island for his stepson, and soon started writing the tales down as a tight narrative. He completed a chapter a day, reading each day's work to the family and friends. In a mere few months he completed *The Sea Cook*, his original title for the book, referring to the novel's charismatic pirate and cook, Long John Silver.

In his essay, "My First Book," about the production of *Treasure Island*, Stevenson proclaims that his intent as to write an adventure story for boys. He was sure of the project's success because he had "a boy at hand to be a touchstone" (his stepson). He also admits that his father was an important contributor: "My father caught fire at once with all the romance and childishness of his original nature." But one of the most significant parts of the essay is Stevenson's discussion of the other books and authors that influenced his writing of *Treasure Island*. Stevenson takes the theoretical stand that no single author can claim as his own an image which is common to a genre:

> No doubt the parrot once belonged to Robinson Crusoe. No doubt the skeleton is conveyed from Poe. I think little of these, they are trifles and details; and no man can hope to have a monopoly of skeletons or make a corner in talking birds. The stockade, I am told, is from Masterman Ready. It may be, I care not a jot. These useful writers had fulfilled the poet's saying: departing they had left behind them Footprints on the sands of time.

Stevenson then goes on to discuss his great debt to Washington Irving, whose *Tales of a Traveller* provided "a good deal of the material detail of my first chapters...all were the property of Washington Irving." With these frank statements, full of conviction, Stevenson tells us plainly that he has followed the footsteps—the images and details that create the atmosphere in the story—left by other writers; he has freely borrowed from the world's literature about pirates and South Sea islands. This borrowing of the essential and recognizable features of other similar stories is perhaps what makes *Treasure Island* the quintessential, most easily recognized pirate story in literature.

Hoist the Jolly Roger

The skull-and-crossbones flag is an instant cue to a reader that pirates are lurking about somewhere. In fact, the Jolly Roger did not always have a skull or crossbones on it—sometimes it was a skeleton, sometimes an hourglass (a reference to the sands of time which run out on all of us, sooner or later!). Whatever the symbol was, the flag was raised before an attack. Rather than signaling "we take no prisoners," the original meaning of the flag was "don't struggle and nobody gets hurt—" in other words, that a ship under attack that did not put up resistance would be treated mercifully. It's only later that the flag became a signal for danger and death—so much so that it's now used on labels to signal poisonous materials!

Treasure Island was originally published in serial form in 1881 in the magazine *Young Folks*. Because of that, Stevenson went to some lengths to leave the reader hanging in suspense to ensure that he'd be back to read the following issue. Although he later made some modifications to the novel-version of *Treasure Island*, it nevertheless retains much of the "end-of-the-chapter" suspense that makes us want to continue turning the pages until we can catch our breath once again.

Characters

Jim Hawkins: the young and adventurous hero of *Treasure Island* who, along with Doctor Livesey, Squire Trelawney, and Captain Smollett, is part of the ship's cabin crew. He is a boy thrust into an adult world of pirates and high seas danger. A boy in a man's role, Jim acts in a way that is both youthful and seasoned well beyond his years. As a boy, Jim is loyal to his protectors: his mother and father, Dr. Livesey, Squire Trelawney, and Captain Smollett. But he also makes the very adult decision to remain loyal to the pirates Billy Bones and Long John Silver when the responsibility for the safety of others is on his shoulders. Likewise, Jim's boyish playfulness and ingenuity allow him to do things that his adult companions cannot: he can run from pirates as in a game of tag, he can escape a stockade and stow away in small places as though he were playing hide-and-seek. But "playing" with the pirates involves very real and grown-up stakes—frequently Jim's own life is in the balance—and "winning" means killing another human being! Jim's role in the story also means changing sides when necessary: first he is the Cabin Boy who takes orders, then he is the captain who gives orders to Israel Hands; he is friend to Long John Silver, then foe, then friend. The youth does what he must to accomplish "the man's job" he has been given.

Jim's multifaceted heroics spark most of the action and intrigue in the story. He has the good sense to take the treasure map in the first place, to keep quiet about what he knows, to relate Silver's plot to the others, and to

HAWKINS, WE ARE DEPENDING ON YOU TO DO A MAN'S JOB.

I'LL DO WHAT I CAN, SIR.

strike deals with Ben Gunn and the pirates to ensure his own safety. By contrast, his adventurous zeal drives him from his comrades and the relative safety of the stockade as he attempts to retake the ship from the pirates. Later he stands up to Silver and the other pirates back in the stockade, becoming their prisoner in the process. But when all is said and done, Jim has come to the rescue of his friends on several occasions, or, as Dr. Livesey puts it to him, "Every step, it's you that saves our lives."

As the cause of most of the novel's action, it is no surprise that Jim is the story's narrator. He has been asked by the Squire and Doctor to "write down the whole particulars about Treasure Island, from the beginning to the end…" and is explicitly trusted to provide a reliable report. Again, young Jim has been given an adult task to perform. He does it well. It is his description of his own experience of fear and danger in the midst of his adventures that creates the edge-of-your-seat reading that is *Treasure Island*.

Long John Silver: the one-legged ship's cook and leader of the pirates. Silver's cruelty and brutality earn him respect and fear from the other pirates. But he also possesses irresistible and dangerous charm and shrewdly uses it to fool everyone for his benefit. Unlike other pirates, Silver has had some education and can "speak like a book when so minded" (Chapter 10). Like an actor, he uses this talent to seduce the trust of the Doctor, the Squire, and Jim Hawkins early in the voyage—the Squire goes so far as to exclaim, "The man's a perfect trump!" and trusts him more than the ship's captain. It is only after his treacherous plot is discovered that Silver's true nature is revealed. But among the pirates Silver continues his manipulations. Even when given the black spot (a death sentence) by his fellow mutineers, Silver skillfully talks his way out of danger and, demonstrating his powers of psychology and rhetoric, manages to make the others beg to have him back as captain.

Ultimately, those who were once determined to kill him shout "Silver for captain!" and "Silver forever!"

Doctor Livesey: the intelligent and respected physician who helps even the ill pirates when necessary. The Doctor puts his professional duty above all else, but does not hesitate to bravely stand up to Billy Bones and other pirates. He shows great concern for Jim Hawkins, and recognizes Jim's achievements in saving his life. It is Doctor Livesey who comes up with the final plan to escape the pirates and rescue the treasure.

Squire Trelawney: a wealthy and trusting aristocrat who initiates the voyage for the treasure, appointing himself "admiral." The Squire relies on his first impressions, and is easily deceived by Long John Silver's initial charm. in spite of being somewhat stuffy and overly romantic about the sea, the Squire is courageous and the best shot among those who oppose the pirates. But he's also unimaginative and dangerously confident in his own "leadership" by right of his social position, easily impressed by someone who appears to respect his position (Silver), and as easily annoyed by someone who questions his judgment (Captain Smollett).

Captain Smollett: the captain of the ship *Hispaniola*. A professional and disciplined leader, the Captain is the first to suspect Long John Silver and his mates of shady intentions. Although he first seems gruff to the Squire, the Captain proves himself a man of good judgment. His early strategy for dealing with the mutineers allows the others to reach safety in the stockade on the island.

Billy Bones: the first pirate encountered in the story. Bones is a heavy-drinking and mean-spirited man hiding at the Admiral Benbow Inn from Long John Silver's pirates. He has the map of Treasure Island. Like Silver,

Real Pirates

Robert Louis Stevenson was drawing on an established tradition of pirate tales when he wrote *Treasure Island*—but many of those tales were grounded in fact. Piracy has been with us since mankind first ventured out onto the sea in boats—much of it a part of normal warfare between seafaring nations. The characters we think of as "pirates"—like Long John Silver and his mates—were often part of an informal non-military force that harried and harassed the ships of other nations. Under Elizabeth I of England, when war between Spain and England was an off-again on-again proposition (mostly on-again), private ships carried "Letters of Marque," essentially a license to attack, loot and destroy any ship sailing under the flag of the enemy, military or not. These ships—and the folk who sailed them—were called privateers.

What made a privateer different from a pirate? A privateer attacked the ships of the enemy (and maybe, occasionally, the ships of a neutral nation, but that was rather bad form). A pirate attacked anyone. They both made their money the same way: by taking whatever goods and prisoners they could. The romantic tradition is that privateers were in some way more honorable—treated their prisoners more tenderly, didn't harm women, behaved on the whole rather like Errol Flynn: swashbuckling, but honorable. But in truth there probably wasn't an enormous difference between privateers and pirates except that all-important Letter of Marque. There were probably some honorable pirates...but the ones we remember are the *vicious* ones:

Blackbeard (born Edward Teach, probably in Bristol, England) was one of the most brutal and feared of the West Indies pirates. Tales of his cruelty to captives (and to his crew members) spread across the Caribbean up to, and after, his death in 1718.

Sir Henry Morgan, a Welshman by birth, spent much of his pirate career harrying the Spanish in the Caribbean, until he was accused of attacks against English forces as well. He was captured, brought back to England for trial—and pardoned by King Charles II, who not only believed in his innocence of the charges, but knighted him and appointed him Lieutenant Governor of Jamaica as well!

Jean Lafitte was born in France in 1780, but emigrated to New Orleans with his brother Pierre. Lafitte kept his pirate headquarters near the city, from which he struck all over the Caribbean (returning to New Orleans to fence the spoils through his brother's shop!). During the War of 1812 he was approached by the British, who wanted him to help them defeat the American forces at New Orleans. He not only refused, but warned the American forces, and became a hero at the Battle of New Orleans. He tried going straight, but eventually returned to the sea and his buccaneering ways.

Billy Bones strikes a deal with Jim Hawkins in an attempt to secure his safety.

Black Dog: the first pirate sent to take the map from Billy Bones.

Blind Pew: the beggar who was once a member of the crew of the famous Captain Flint, the murderous pirate whose treasure is buried on Treasure Island. Pew delivers the "black spot" to Bones, signifying that Bones is marked for death.

Ben Gunn: a pirate who has been marooned on Treasure Island for three years. He knows where the treasure is, and offers to help Jim and the others in exchange for being rescued from the island.

Israel Hands: one of Silver's vicious sailors. Hands tries to kill Jim after Jim saves his life.

Plot

What kind of novel is *Treasure Island*? At times it is a mystery; at other times it is closer to a horror story. Above all it resembles a thriller. For Stevenson, it is clearly and simply a novel of adventure. In his essay "A Humble Remonstrance," Stevenson explains the simplified style of his novel to the skeptical writer Henry James. Stevenson argues that for a boy reading his story,

...a pirate is a beard, a pair of wide trousers and a liberal complement of pistols...in this elementary novel of adventure, the characters need to be presented with but one class of qualities— the warlike and formidable... danger is the matter with which this class of novel deals; fear, the passion with which it idly trifles, and the characters are portrayed only so far as they realize the

sense of danger and provoke the sympathy of fear.

For Stevenson, deep psychology and difficult symbolism are unnecessary when the subject is treasure. Instead, the necessary elements are pistols and swords, eye patches and peg legs, treasure chests and skeletons. (See previous page.) These are the things that the reader immediately recognizes as belonging to a certain type of story involving danger on the high seas—they are signs that announce to the reader: "pirates." Stevenson assumes that the reader will recognize such key images and understand what kind of story *Treasure Island* is meant to be. In other words, when we read "Yo-ho-ho and a bottle of rum" coming from the mouth of a man with a saber cut across his cheek, we prepare ourselves for a pirate adventure.

Stevenson doesn't overdo it though, or rely excessively on clichés of piratehood to achieve the effects of the book. He limits the imagery to just enough that we easily understand the context of the events. One can even say that Stevenson strips away as many expected elements as he includes. For example, with the exception of the marooned Ben Gunn, the island holds no other inhabitants—no savages or wild animals—to interfere with the plot. Likewise, no one luckily happens upon supplies of food and ammunition left by previous visitors, and no rescuers arrive to jump into the fray. The plot of *Treasure Island* is built from the limited number of characters aboard the Hispaniola (and Ben Gunn) and centers on a single intent: finding the treasure. This is why Stevenson calls his story a "pure" adventure.

We naturally bring a storehouse of stereotypical images to this and every novel we read, and the novel uses them to help us along in our understanding. The reader knows who is evil and who is not, and can thereby anticipate the danger and fear in the story. But Stevenson

LISTEN, MOTHER, I HEAR THE TAPPING OF A BLIND MAN'S CANE DOWNSTAIRS. TAKE THE MONEY AND LET'S BE GOING!

I'LL JUST TAKE WHAT IS OWED ME AND NOT A BIT OVER!

provides the necessary action, the twists and turns that place mystery and fear at a precise place in the tale. In *Treasure Island* Stevenson's chief mechanism for this is Jim Hawkins. Jim is present at the most tense and pivotal moment in the story: the attempted murder of Billy Bones and the discovery of the map (see previous page); the discovery of Silver's plot; the discovery of Ben Gunn; retaking the ship from the pirates; the killing Israel Hands; being captured in the enemy's camp. These are hardly the typical problems a boy deals with. With Jim as the narrator, the reader experiences a boy's fears in the face of grown-up dangers. We experience the danger as Jim does.

Further, it is by virtue of Jim's double, boy-like and man-like

Pirates on Stage and Screen

There's something about pirate stories that makes wonderful movies—all that swash, all that buckle, the sails fluttering in the breeze, the flash of cutlasses clashing in battle.... There have been at least four film versions of *Treasure Island*:

- The 1934 *Treasure Island* starred character actor Wallace Beery as Long John Silver.
- The 1950 *Treasure Island* from Walt Disney is considered by many to be the best, with Robert Newton the "defining" Long John; when this *Treasure Island* was re-released in 1975 some of its more violent scenes were edited out, but the film has been restored and is available on tape or laser disc.
- In 1972 the great Orson Welles played Long John Silver in a version of *Treasure Island* he also co-scripted.
- In 1992 a made-for-cable *Treasure Island* aired with Charlton Heston playing against type (quite successfully) as the charismatic Long John. This one had Oliver Reed in a brief appearance as Billy Bones, and Christopher Lee as Blind Pew!

It doesn't stop there, of course. There have been dozens of pirate movies—serious and tongue-in-cheek—since movies began, from films about historical pirates (like Sir Henry Morgan in *Morgan*, and Jean Lafitte in *The Buccaneers*), to musicals (like the Gilbert and Sullivan romp *The Pirates of Penzance* and the 1948 Judy Garland/Gene Kelly film *The Pirate*), to swashbuckling adventures like *Captain Blood*, with Errol Flynn, Basil Rathbone and Olivia deHaviland (who teamed up again in *Robin Hood*). In recent years there have been a few forays into pirate-dom, notably *Pirates* (with Walter Matthau) and *Cutthroat Island* with Geena Davis. And no list of film pirates would be complete without mentioning *Captain Hook*, first in various versions of *Peter Pan*, and then in *Hook* itself, where the great pirate was played by Dustin Hoffman.

perspectives, that the book becomes both a pirate adventure story and a chronicle of a tragedy of sorts. This comes from Jim's two paradoxical attitudes to his own tale. On the one hand the voyage is like a daydream of adventure and treasure: "And I was going to sea myself, to sea in a schooner, with a piping boatswain, and pig-tailed singing seamen, to sea, bound for an unknown island, and to seek for buried treasures!" (Chapter 7). On the other hand, his memory has a far more real and serious tinge to it: "…but in all my fancies nothing occurred to me so strange and tragic as our actual adventures." (Chapter 7). Jim sees, for a young boy (even a young boy when death was a more commonplace part of life) a lot of cruelty, fear, and death.

I'LL FINISH 'EM ALL OFF WHEN WE'VE GOT THE BLUNT ON BOARD. WE'VE GOT TO WAIT OUR TIME. HERE'S CAPTAIN SMOLLETT TO SAIL THE SHIP FOR US...HERE'S THE SQUIRE AND DOCTOR WITH A MAP TO FIND THE STUFF AND HELP US GET IT ABOARD! ONLY ONE THING I CLAIM...I CLAIM TRELAWNEY, AND I'LL WRING HIS NECK OFF WITH THESE HANDS OF MINE.

Themes

Intention and Choice

It is difficult to read *Treasure Island* and not be reminded of other "island" stories involving shipwrecked voyagers. Johann Wyss's *The Swiss Family Robinson* and, of course, Daniel Defoe's *Robinson Crusoe*, come immediately to mind. But in *Treasure Island* the themes of colonialism—establishment, settlement, Christian-ization, the "noble savage," and so forth—are absent. Both pirates and cabin crew want to get to the island, get what they came for, and get away again! There is no attempt to turn the island into another Europe based on a common set of laws and rules. *Treasure Island* is a story of greed and desire; the allure of the island comes simply from the treasure buried there. The journey serves pragmatic ends: for the pirates, it's a matter of business—they want the treasure; for the others, although they too are initially driven by a desire for riches, the journey is ultimately a source of adventure: "Hang the treasure! It's the glory of the sea that has turned my head," writes Trelawney in a letter to the Doctor (Chapter 7).

Clearly both groups want the treasure, but their reasons for wanting it are not necessarily the same.

The pirates are motivated by far less noble intentions than the cabin crew, and it is this initial distinction between the two groups that grows throughout the story and becomes its thematic basis. Instead of facing threats from native islanders or "outsiders," the characters of *Treasure Island* must battle disorder and criminality which originate from within their own group. In Stevenson's stripped down "pure" adventure, the environment of Treasure Island exerts no influence or control over the moral decision making of the treasure hunters. The island, completely separated from all that is British and from any common authority, is a morally neutral territory. While on the island, all participants—pirates and cabin crew alike—are free to act in whatever manner they choose. The outcome of events depends only on free choice.

Power

The absence of a commonly recognized authority, or leader, is thematically important throughout the novel. In *Treasure Island* power does not simply exist as a given (and people who rely on the customary authority of rank—Squire Trelawney, for example—may be surprised to find that authority suddenly *gone*). In this book power does not belong to anyone for very long. Rather, it moves continuously from one person to another. The ship provides a notable example of this: before the Hispaniola sets sail, we learn that Silver, the cook, has had a hand in selecting the crew, rather than Trelawney, who is, after all, in charge of the voyage. Aboard ship there is an immediate split in authority between Captain Smollett, Trelawney, and Silver, each suspicious of the other's power and judgment. On the island there is an obvious rift in authority between the pirates and the cabin crew, with each group battling the other and proclaiming its right—its authority—to possess the treasure. There is a similar conflict among the pirates themselves, when Silver's fellow pirates attempt to depose him as captain of the mutineers.

The hierarchy of power—

which at first is clear and "natural"—is eventually turned on its head, and the possession of power is completely subverted: the admiral, Trelawney, gradually loses his authority to the point that he has little significance in any of the action at the end of the story. Most striking is the case of the cabin boy, Jim Hawkins, who assumes the title of captain as he takes the ship from Israel Hands, and Long John Silver, who reveals himself to be the powerful and ruthless mastermind behind the mutiny, rather than a genial one-legged cook. This blurring of authority provides the instability and unpredictability that propels the novel's action. Thematically, these conflicts of power establish the basis for the novel's unending clashes of good and evil. There is a collapse of the boundary between law and order, civilization and barbarity—to the extent that a distinction between such terms becomes increasingly difficult. Is it "evil" that Jim must kill a man in order to save his own life and those of his companions? How is the order imposed on the cabin crew by Captain Smollett more "civilized" than the pirates' internal order? Is Jim really "treasonous" for leaving the stockade?

These questions point to one of the most provocative themes in the novel: the ability of an individual to radically change his behavior and alliances according to his changing needs (and the moral value of this sort of adaptability). The society that takes shape on Treasure Island is chaotic; it is guided by individual pursuits concerned with financial gain. There is no sense of permanent community of common good. Stevenson paints a bleak picture of human nature as it wanders unchecked in pursuit of wealth.

Role Models on the Road to Manhood

There is, buried within this chaos, the particular case of Jim Hawkins. Jim is present at the very first instance of power exchange and its resulting instability. When Billy Bones arrives at the Admiral Benbow Inn he challenges the authority of Jim's father. Not only does Bones disrupt the tranquillity of the inn, but he even steals some of Jim's own loyalty from his dying father, hiring the boy

to keep watch for him, becoming a glamorous, albeit slightly scary, figure. By the time the voyage begins, Jim is without a father and separated from his mother. He has only those on board the ship to look up to and use as a model for his passage to manhood. Here lies another of the novel's most prominent themes: the progression from innocence to maturity; the transformation from boy to man. Jim's voyage takes him away from the safety of home and family and into an adventurous world of total freedom, before he returns home again, a changed individual. While Jim's motives remain honest throughout the story, he nevertheless must choose from among the various moral role models offered by the opposing parties, and decide for himself how to act.

Jim is initiated by none other than Billy Bones, who brings danger and adventure to Jim's very doorstep, to the inn where Jim lives and works. In spite of the "fearful stories" Bones tells (or perhaps because of them) Jim's imagination is sparked by his presence, and Jim believes in retrospect that "it was a fine excitement in a quiet country life…." (Chapter 1). Jim's daydream of discovery is further propelled by the treasure map, which he pores over, memorizing every detail. Jim imagines "savages" and "dangerous animals" like the ones found in stories about pirates and exotic South Sea islands. What he cannot imagine is that the true danger will come from pirates like Bones himself. But in the beginning, pirates offer Jim an adventurous escape, and Silver's additional charm makes him look like a loyal, if colorful, companion. This image of pirates and their later treachery account for their ambiguous status in *Treasure Island*. On the one hand, they're cast in a light of wonder and admiration— they're figures of romance. On the other, they appear as figures of fear, vicious and depraved. Thus Jim is able to say of Silver that he is "the best of possible shipmates" (Chapter 8) and yet, later "I had…taken such a horror of his cruelty, duplicity, and power, that I could scarcely conceal a shudder when he laid his hand upon my arm" (Chapter 12). And yet, in the end, Jim cannot help but admire the strength and courage of Silver in spite of his duplicity. "The work that man went through, leaping on his crutch 'til the muscles of his chest were fit to burst, was work no sound man ever equaled" (Chapter 33).

The masculine and adventurous qualities of the pirates account for Jim's refusal to reject them as models. The pirates are cunning, adventurous, rash, gutsy, and tricky. They are counterparts to the contemplative, logical, loyal, and moral qualities of the cabin crew. (It's intriguing to consider the two groups in terms of Stevenson's own personal experience—his family, strictly religious, logical, mathematical engineers—and the artists and writers with whom he spent much of his time—imaginative, adventurous, far less conventional. Clearly Stevenson saw the good in both "models," for neither he, nor his hero, rejects either one outright.)

Jim demonstrates a willingness to experiment with all of these traits. He is the only person who goes between these two groups with ease and gains the trust of each: "Jim can help us more than anyone. The men are not shy with him," says the Doctor. Furthermore, the decisions that guide Jim's actions reflect the competing influences that surround him: protecting the stockade, returning to the stockade, and keeping his word to Silver are actions that reflect the influence of the cabin crew.

Sneaking on shore, leaving the stockade to retake the ship, and killing Israel Hands—these are more independent, pirate-like actions.

With this duality, Jim resembles one of his shipmates more than the others: Long John Silver. Silver too exhibits a dual nature which, like Jim, allows him to go between opposing groups by earning the trust of the cabin crew as well as the respect of the other pirates. Silver recognizes and respects Jim's honor and fearlessness, qualities which make him a reflection of the pirate himself as a young man. Silver openly admits as much when he notes that Jim is "the picter of my own self when I was young and handsome" (Chapter 28). The crucial implication here is that Silver sees in Jim as good a pirate as he does a gentleman. What guarantees that Jim will be a gentleman is his ability to absorb only the admirable qualities in Silver, minus the barbaric cruelty. These qualities allow Jim to master his surroundings and make things happen by asserting his individuality and free will. From Silver, Jim learns, essentially, to be a leader.

If the story and themes of *Treasure Island* sound familiar—even if this is the first time you are reading it—they should. *Treasure Island*'s uniqueness and place in literary history is a result of Robert Louis Stevenson's vivid, action-packed narrative. Indeed, it is considered the best example of its kind in the genre. Its specificity aside, however, there exists something much more fundamental at the heart of this novel, something we all recognize. We see it in *Star Wars*, *Raiders of the Lost Ark*, *T2*, television programs, scores of literary works from *The Odyssey* to *Lord of the Flies*, and in countless other cultural artifacts and settings. This "pure adventure" story is the eternal story of the battle of good and evil in faraway places. One can think of *Treasure Island* as one version of the classic Medieval hero's journey or quest, in which a youth leaves home, faces perils, slays a dragon, and returns a hero (and a man). In the same way, *Star Wars* could be considered a "rewriting" of *Treasure Island*, and it comes as no surprise that when the conflict is between right and wrong, we feel as comfortable on Treasure Island as we do in outer space.

In fact, some early critics considered that *Treasure Island* was not appropriate children's literature at all because it lacked a "moral lesson." The book was, after all, published at a time when the majority of fiction for children was supposed to be morally improving, and often took the form of thinly disguised (and stickily sentimental) sermons. Perhaps the moral lesson of *Treasure Island* lies in watching Jim Hawkins find his way through a confusing moral landscape, taking on the traits which serve him best, whether they come from the cabin crew or the pirates. The "rite of passage" tale is, in fact, always a story about finding your own strengths and choosing your own "right behaviors."

Such an historical perspective casts some doubt on Stevenson's assertion that *Treasure Island* is "a story for boys," and that "women were excluded." In what way is *Treasure Island* more a story for male children than, say, *Star Wars*? The fact is, no gender or age group can stake a claim to a pure adventure story like this. For ultimately, what makes *Treasure Island* a classic is its appeal to a fundamental human attraction: in a pure adventure story we are all adventurers.

Study Questions

- Stevenson freely admitted that certain images and ideas in *Treasure Island* could be found in stories he read before he wrote the book. Is it possible for an author not to borrow from other sources? What does it mean to be original? What makes *Treasure Island* original?

- *Treasure Island* was originally published in serial form; if you were to publish the Classics Illustrated adaptation of the book now, where would you end each installment?

- How does Long John Silver earn the trust of Trelawney and the rest of the cabin crew? How does he earn the respect of the other pirates? Is there a difference in his actions, manner or speech when he is with each of the groups?

- How might Silver's handicap be an advantage for him? Can it give a false impression of his abilities? Is Long John Silver more or less dangerous than the other pirates?

- People in *Treasure Island* are always striking deals with each other, from the seemingly harmless (when Billy Bones promises Jim fourpence for each month he keeps watch for a one-legged man) to the deadly serious (when Silver bargains for his life and future with the cabin crew). What "deals" can you think of in the book? Which ones are smart bargains?

- As a reader, what are the advantages and disadvantages of knowing that a story comes from a particular genre? Knowing that *Treasure Island* is a pirate story, do we immediately predict the events and outcome of the story? Is there still suspense? What preconceptions and images do you bring to it? Can you think of other genres (i.e., mystery, science fiction) where you might bring a set of expectations, even a specialized vocabulary, with you?

•Power—who has it and who loses it—is a hidden theme in *Treasure Island*. Consider obvious authority figures like Doctor Livesey, Captain Smollett, and Squire Trelawney. Are they always in command? Once they lose their authority, can they regain it? And how does an *un*-obvious authority figure like Long John Silver gain—and maintain—his command?

•On Treasure Island, people are free to act as they like, without rules and punishment to stop them. How does Stevenson depict human nature under these "natural" conditions? Do you agree that this is how people would behave under the same circumstances?

•How does Billy Bones become a kind of father figure for Jim? Who are Jim's other father figures in this story? If you had to chose one as a "mentor," which would it be?

•What are John Silver's admirable qualities? What about the other pirates? What are negative qualities in the Doctor, Trelawney, and the Captain? Does a role model have to be perfect (consider some of today's role models—sports and entertainment figures) or can we filter out that which is admirable from that which isn't?

•What do you think makes up an adventure story? What stories other than *Treasure Island* can you think of that fit those requirements?

About the Essayist:

Trevor Pickering is a President's Fellow at Columbia University, where he chairs the First Year Undergraduate French program. He is a doctoral candidate at Columbia, where he received an M.A. and an M.Phil.